Selfless Love

Freely Receive.

Freely Give.

Daniel Newton

@ Copyright 2023 Daniel Newton, GP Publishing

www.GracePlaceRedding.com

Contributing authors: Downing McDade, Austin Chappell, Daniel Fagot, Katherine Marx, Elizabeth Newton, and the Grace Place Leadership Team
ISBN: 978-1-957601-07-6

Resources by Daniel Newton and Grace Place Ministries:

Truth in Tension: 55 Days to Living in Balance
Immeasurable: Reviewing the Goodness of God
Never Give Up: The Supernatural Power of Christlike Endurance
The Lost Art of Discipleship
The Lost Art of Discipleship Workbook
The Lost Art of Perseverance
All Things
It Is Finished
The Lost Art of Faith Righteousness
The Lost Art of Fasting
The Lost Art of Selfless Love
GP Music: Beginnings – Worship Album

For more information on these books
and other inspiring resources, visit us at
www.GracePlaceMedia.com

"Love suffers long and is kind; love does not envy; love does not parade itself, is not puffed up; does not behave rudely, does not seek its own, is not provoked, thinks no evil; does not rejoice in iniquity, but rejoices in the truth; bears all things, believes all things, hopes all things, endures all things. Love never fails..."

- *1 Corinthians 13: 4-8*

Table of Contents

Introduction

Love has become an overused word in today's society. We use it for almost everything. We say we "love" pizza. We "love" our favorite movies. We say we "love" sunsets, sports cars, and vacations. Then, sometimes in the same breath, we tell our kids, our spouses, or even God, that we "love" them. Doesn't that seem a little odd? Surely we don't feel the same way about the Lord as we do about the latest blockbuster movie or a slice of pizza.

We live in a culture that has lost connection to what love really is. It's not intentional, but the way we throw around the word "love" makes it lose significance. The more you use a term, the more familiar it becomes. The more familiar it becomes, the less weight it carries.

Love isn't just another good idea like cleaning your room or getting eight hours of sleep. It's not just a feeling, either. It's more than happy thoughts and sunshine. It isn't a hole you can fall into by accident. How many times have you heard someone say, "I fell in love!" No. You don't fall in love; you choose to love. Love certainly, carries emotion, but it's far bigger than that.

Love is the very essence of God's nature. It's who He is. It defines how He interacts with creation, including us. God isn't just *loving*; He *is* love. Because He is love, He *does* loving things. Everything about God's nature reflects an attribute of love.

In the Church today, there's a ministry and a book for every topic under the sun. There are books, ministries, and communities fully devoted just to prayer, prophecy, apologetics, evangelism, fasting, and countless other subjects. These are all important and present in the life of a healthy Christian, but they are only branches of the main theme: God's unconditional love. "And though I have the gift of prophecy, and understand all mysteries and all knowledge, and though I have all faith, so that I could remove mountains, but have not love, I am nothing" (see 1 Cor. 13:2). In other words, you can preach until you're blue in the face, give the best argument for the existence of God, and fast more than anyone else, but if you don't have love, it's all useless.

The central message of the Gospel is that God *loved* the world (see John 3:16). I have met people who talk to me about the importance of various doctrines and how they're missing from the Church today. They will be outspoken about a single issue. However, they are having problems getting along with the people around them. Giftings and revelations are important, but knowing God's love for you and His love toward others must come before everything else.

This book is designed to take us back to the foundation of our faith to rediscover what love truly is. We will be exploring more deeply what it looks like to live a 1 Corinthians 13 lifestyle. Through the teaching and meditations at the end of each chapter, my goal is to awaken within you a desire to love others like Jesus loved. He knew who He was and why He was on the Earth: to express the loving image of the Father.

As His body, we are called to represent God to the world. Yet how can we if we misunderstand His nature? 1 Corinthians 13 says we can be experts in many topics, but if we don't have love first, it's meaningless. Living selflessly has become a lost art, but it doesn't have to be. It's time to go back to the basics and remember how much God loves us and how we are called to love others. It's time that we stop loving based on how we feel from one moment to the next and actually become like Love Himself.

Chapter One

You Act Because You Are

"We love Him, because He first loved us."
- 1 John 4:19

Jesus Christ, the expressed image of God, came to display the eternal love of a good Father. The Cross is the greatest act of love that history has ever recorded. It's more than a story or an historic event. It's an ever-present reality. It's here *now*: the body and blood of a loving Savior. He saw you as being worth His death and resurrection. It's upon the experiential knowledge of this love that we base our salvation.

We cannot give away love that we've never received. We cannot display a God that we've never come face to face with. Becoming love begins with experiencing it. When you recognize and receive the perfect love of God, it changes the entire way you see the world. You will look at every person with a deep conviction: "They are worth it."

It's here, seated in heavenly places (see Eph. 2:6), that you can finally know who you are. You are righteous because He says you are. You are holy because He says you are. You are pure because He says you are. When you believe this, it will change your behavior. It wipes away the consciousness of sin as though it were a dry-erase marker on a whiteboard. The purpose of Jesus' life, death, and resurrection wasn't to fix the mess you had become. He came to die for you because He sees you as worth far more than you can imagine.

"Who Am I?"

One of the most important questions we need to ask daily is, "Who am I? To live a lifestyle of selfless love, we *must* know that we are the righteousness of God. We cannot live like Christ without believing that God has lovingly done everything necessary to make us holy in His sight. We have not been merely forgiven; we have been brought into union with God through the power of the Holy Spirit. Our primary focus should be to get to the point where we confidently know we are no longer sinners.

The consciousness of sin clouds the water of our convictions. If you believe you are impure, you will look at others through the lens of impurity. If you believe you are unforgivable, you will find it difficult to forgive others as well. Many of us still struggle with thoughts like, "I'm a sinner because I did this and this and this!" If we are constantly battling with sin, we won't have the time to look outside ourselves and love others.

We have to get to a place where we know that just because we do something wrong or make a mistake, it doesn't define who we are. What God says defines us. When you were born, you were born a sinner. You sinned because you were a sinner. You didn't sin first and *then* become a sinner. The same applies to righteousness. Righteousness begins in your beliefs and manifests in your actions. When we act according to who the Lord says we are, we will manifest God's love toward others.

For example, in John 8, Jesus was presented with a woman caught in the act of adultery. Everyone was prepared to stone her except Jesus. He said, "Let he who is without sin cast the first stone." One by one, they all dropped their stones. "Woman, where are those that condemn you?... Neither do I condemn you; go and sin no more" (see John 8:2-11).

There is a valuable truth hidden in this story. Even when caught in the middle of the sin of adultery, Jesus did not condemn her. That is a radical demonstration of both love and mercy. The presence of Jesus evicts condemnation. In the absence of condemnation is the power to live righteously.

As I mentioned earlier, the Father's great love for us caused Him to send his Son to die for our forgiveness. When we talk about God's righteousness, we must understand that His righteousness is shown through His love. When we know who we are, we have the power to do the same.

Meditation

"But God shows his love for us, because while we were still sinners Christ died for us. So, now that we have been made righteous by his blood, we can be even more certain that we will be saved from God's wrath through him."

- Romans 5:8-9 (CEB)

Take a moment to meditate on Romans 5:8-9. Because of His great love, you have been made righteous. You are free from sin and saved from wrath and punishment. Knowing that you have been forgiven of all your sin, how does that make you think about others in your life? You may feel the need to repent for living with a consciousness of your own sin. Let the truth of His love and forgiveness wash those areas clean. It's time to think of yourself as being holy in Christ. What will you do differently as this revelation begins to come alive?

Chapter Two

Responding in Love

Responding in love goes beyond our actions. Love isn't measured by our deeds alone. You can do good things, but have selfish intentions. You can also do bad things with good intentions. Love begins in the heart and produces an authentic response. "For God so loved the world that He gave His only begotten Son, that whoever believes in Him should not perish but have everlasting life" (John 3:16). Because God loved us, He gave what was necessary (His Son), so that we could have an eternal relationship with Him.

Responding in love looks like responding as Christ would. Responding as Christ would comes from our understanding that He lives in and through us. This comes through believing the truth of the Word. "For the love of Christ compels us, because we judge thus: that if One died for all, then all died" (2 Cor. 5:14).

Jesus' sacrifice changed everything. No longer do we look at people according to their performance, their efforts, or their good and bad deeds. We look at them according to Christ's love. Christ's love took Him to a cross to sacrifice himself for the good of many. He died to forgive every person of his or her trespasses. His love, by it's very nature is sacrificial. While many haven't or won't accept this, it remains our responsibility as His body to treat them following the words of Christ: "Forgive them Father, they know not what they do." (see Luke 23:34)

If you've been alive for more than a few years you've experienced someone doing something that hurts you. They may have lied about you, stolen from you, or worse. However, when people treat us poorly, we are called to return good to them. When people speak poorly of us, the Father's desire is that we would bless them. We are not called to give an eye for an eye or a tooth for a tooth. The message of God's love displayed through Jesus is to overcome evil by doing good (Rom. 12:21). You always have the choice to be offended. However, even in the most unfair of circumstances, there is always an invitation to respond in love.

Love is Not Self-Seeking

1 Corinthians 13:5 says, "Love is not self-seeking." We can read that and think, *Oh, it's not that big of a deal.* However, some of the biggest tensions we face are: *Is it about me, or is it about God? Is it about me, or is it about others? Is it about what I want, or is it about what others want?* When we understand that love is not self-seeking, we can't make it about ourselves. We have been called to be love, and love is not selfish.

We have to stop getting offended. That sounds like a difficult statement to live up to but think about it. If I'm getting offended, I'm making it about how something is affecting me... but love never makes a big deal about itself. Love always focuses on the other person. Love doesn't lead you to focus on your pain or

your offense. That would make it about you!

We say, "Well, you made me feel like this, and I'm hurting because you did this." We get so focused on ourselves and our hurt that we don't learn to love others. Then, we put a demand on somebody else we claim to love and say, "Here's what you need to do to make me feel better." The last time I checked, we're supposed to love others *regardless* of whether they love us back or not. C.S. Lewis once said, "Love is never wasted, for its value does not rest upon reciprocity." We make so many things about ourselves that we don't even understand love anymore.

Let's use an example: There's a couple in your church, and the news breaks that the husband has been having an affair with another woman. What would be the average reaction? Everyone crowds around the woman and says things like, "Oh my gosh, I'm so sorry! How could that jerk do that to you? He's so evil; he's so wrong." And then we walk up to the husband and say things like, "How could you do that? I can't believe you. You're ruining her life, your life, and your kids' lives." This may seem like a natural, normal reaction. However, this is a common, worldly response.

Who had the affair? Who was deceived to the point of breaking their covenant with their lawfully-wedded spouse? Was it the wife? No! The husband was clearly hurting and broken, too. He was the one looking for love in all the wrong places. We are compassionate toward the woman who didn't do anything wrong, which is good. But we should also be hurting for the man who was so deceived that he stepped outside of his identity and chose sin!

We cast out the person who did something wrong instead of hurting for them. We make a victim out of the woman who was hurt. Should we still love the broken and hurting woman? Yes, of course! She needs all the support she can get. However, we need to get to a place where it's not about one person at the expense of the other. We should desire both people to be spiritually and emotionally restored. Love looks beyond its own preconceived opinions and ideas to seek out what is true. We don't have to settle for partial outcomes. When we awaken to love, we walk in the power to see the true ministry of reconciliation at work. Authentic, selfless love is supernatural. Worldly, natural love could never live up to the task!

Love is Supernatural

"Though I speak with the tongues of men and of angels, but have not love, I have become sounding brass or a clanging cymbal. And though I have the gift of prophecy, and understand all mysteries and all knowledge, and though I have all faith, so that I could remove mountains, but have not love, I am nothing."

- 1 Corinthians 13:1-2

What if you understood every mystery? What if every person you prayed for was instantly healed? What if there wasn't anything you couldn't do? Walking in that level of power would be amazing, right? There is just one problem. According to Scripture, all the faith, miracles, and prophecies in the world can't take the place of love.

As believers, we believe miracles, healings, and prophecy are the ultimate signs of manifesting Christ. However, the Bible says, "If I have the gift of prophecy, if I understand all mysteries... but have not love, I am nothing." The true ultimate display of God's power is love. Without love, the miracles are empty.

In a culture that pursues the supernatural, we need to pull back the reins and remember that love is the most important thing. You can prophesy all you want, get words of knowledge, and perform the craziest miracles, but if we're not walking in love, what does it matter? According to 1 Corinthians, it doesn't.

"And though I bestow all my goods to feed the poor, and though I give my body to be burned, but have not love, it profits me nothing."
- 1 Corinthians 13:3

Even martyrdom without love has no purpose. If we are not walking in love and if we are not becoming love, it means nothing. We were created in the image of God, which is the image of love. Isaiah 60:1 doesn't say, "arise and reflect." It says, "arise and shine." We are not reflecting the glory of God on the earth; we *are* His glory revealed to the world! We are called to display Christlike love because, at the root of who we are, love is shining forth!

"Love suffers long and is kind; love does not envy; love does not parade itself, is not puffed up;"
- 1 Corinthians 13:4

Who wants to suffer long? But that's what love does! It's not about us. It's not about *our* fun, and it's not about what *we* want to do. Love is solely about giving my time, resources, and energy for the sake of others.

Love "is not puffed up." It's not trying to seek attention selfishly. Love is not shouting, "Hey! Look at all the great things I have done!" Love looks past yourself and your personal needs to focus on the individual in front of you. It's tempting for us to boast about our accomplishments or great acts, saying, "Guess what testimony I have and what a great miracle worker I am! Hey, leader, look at me!" But love rejoices in the testimony of another for the sake of the person who was transformed.

"[Love] does not behave rudely, does not seek its own, is not provoked, thinks no evil;"

- 1 Corinthians 13:5

In addition to love not being selfish, love "thinks no evil." Once, I met someone who had known Pastor Bill Johnson from Bethel Church for over 20 years. I asked them this question, "What is the biggest thing you've learned from Bill?" The answer surprised me. They said, "In over 20 years of knowing Bill, I've never heard him say anything negative about anyone." That blew my mind. How many of us struggle to go even a week without saying something negative about someone? But that's love. It thinks no evil!

God is love. He thinks no evil about us. He believes the best about us. He sees the potential in us, and we're called to do this with every person we come into contact with. Every person we meet should see Love through us.

"[Love] does not rejoice in iniquity, but rejoices in the truth;"

- 1 Corinthians 13:6

Love does not rejoice in iniquity. And yet, so many times, I have heard believers say, "Well, that evangelist was just a crook after all. I always knew he was a bad man. I'm glad he's going to jail. He deserves it." Love doesn't rejoice in iniquity! It rejoices in the truth, and the truth leads to freedom.

14

"[Love] bears all things, believes all things, hopes all things, endures all things. Love never fails. But whether there are prophecies, they will fail; whether there are tongues, they will cease; whether there is knowledge, it will vanish away."

- 1 Corinthians 13:7-8

When other spiritual gifts fail, love endures. Even when we don't know what else we can do for someone, we can always love. We can have all the prophetic giftings, be fluent in other tongues, and have tons of spiritual knowledge. However, without a foundation in love, none of these things matter. A prophetic word given without love can carry the spirit of religion. Tongues spoken without love will not endure. Knowledge without love only puffs up. Love is the substance that makes the Christian life function. Without it, we truly have nothing. This is why we need to come back to the foundational truth: "the greatest of these is love."

Meditation

"Love does not traffic in shame and disrespect, nor selfishly seek its own honor. Love is not easily irritated or quick to take offense."

- 1 Corinthians 13:5 (TPT)

Take a few minutes to meditate on this verse. Think of all the ways that God has selflessly pursued, loved, and given to you. When you see His heart, you can begin to manifest it in your own life. Jesus only did what He saw the Father doing (see John 5:19). This should be true for us as well.

While you're meditating, the Spirit may reveal areas in your own life that have been tainted with selfishness. If this begins to happen, allow yourself to repent and change your mind. He is showing this to you not to condemn you but to show you an area where you can walk in the fullness of your true identity.

The Lord may bring someone to mind you need to apologize to for treating them selfishly. If so, write down their name(s) and make a plan to talk to them this week. Follow the Lord in this and ask Him to change you from the inside out. This isn't a shameful thing. It's a fruit of Him changing your heart.

Chapter Three

Love is Generous

Love, by its very nature, gives. A generous heart is a loving heart. God is love, and when we are generous with our time, money, and energy, we are being like Him. When we give to others, it causes a response. Generosity creates generosity. Let me illustrate:

"One day Elisha went to Shunem. And a well-to-do woman was there, who urged him to stay for a meal. So whenever he came by, he stopped there to eat. She said to her husband, 'I know that this man who often comes our way is a holy man of God. Let's make a small room on the roof and put in it a bed and a table, a chair and a lamp for him. Then he can stay there whenever he comes to us.'"
- 2 Kings 4:8-10 (NIV)

Elisha was passing through Shunem. A woman invited him to her house for a meal to bless him. From then on, whenever he would come through town, she would show honor and respect by hosting him for a meal. That's some incredible kindness on its own, but she wanted to do more. One day, she was pondering

17

what else she could do to bless this man of God, and she had this idea: *Let's build a room in our house just for him. That way, whenever he comes into town, he has a place to stay and rest.* This woman went far beyond the bounds of what we would consider normal kindness. That's radical generosity!

One day, Elisha was laying on the bed in the room the Shunammite woman had built for him, pondering this woman's kindness. As he lay there, he became convinced that he needed to do something in return for her—something just as extravagant as the gift she had given him.

> *"What can be done for her?' Elisha asked.*
> *Gehazi said, 'She has no son, and her husband is old.'*
> *Then Elisha said, 'Call her.' So he called her, and she stood in the doorway. 'About this time next year,' Elisha said, 'you will hold a son in your arms.' 'No, my lord!' she objected. 'Please, man of God, don't mislead your servant!' But the woman became pregnant, and the next year about that same time she gave birth to a son, just as Elisha had told her."*
> *- 2 Kings 4:14-17 (NIV)*

This woman had a desire so near to her heart the thought of it not coming to pass felt like it might break her. She had a dream to have a child. When she decided to go out of her way to wildly bless Elisha, God decided to wildly bless her. To put it another way, the love she expressed toward Elisha released a generous response back from heaven.

Love is radical because God is radical. When we partner with love in blessing someone, we are partnering with God's nature. God *does* many amazing things, but God *is* love. As we join with God in releasing generosity to those around us, it has radical results for both those receiving and giving.

A remarkable example of this kind of love can be found in the life of Pastor Rodney Howard-Browne of Revival Ministries International. A couple of years ago, I was at his Spring Ministers conference with some of my team, where he shared the following testimony.

In 2001, Pastor Rodney had been in a season of almost non-stop travel and was exhausted. That year he traveled to 60 cities all over the world. After his Winter Camp Meetings, he found himself trying to figure out, "How am I going to reach the world from here?" Around this time, Reinhard Bonke came and visited Pastor Rodney at his home in Tampa, Florida. While there, Reinhard shared how in that year, they had led 10 million people to the Lord. Pastor Rodney went on to find out that Reinhard was planning to move from Germany to America. Immediately Pastor Rodney was reminded of the story of the Shunamite, perceiving this was a holy man of God. Without even consulting his wife, he offered to give Reinhard his home.

"I am going to give you my house."

Reinhard responded, "Thank you, but I don't need to be in Tampa. I need to be in Orlando."

Pastor Rodney said, "Ok, then we'll get you a house there!"

"I don't want to buy one." He replied.

"It doesn't matter; we'll rent one! You pick a nice area and a nice house."

Later Pastor Rodney realized that Reinhard would need furniture with his new home. So he lavishly filled the house with everything he would need. Then he thought Reinhard is going to need a car. So pastor Rodney went to a BMW dealership, bought him a brand new BMW 740Li, and put it in his garage.

When Evangelist Bonnke moved in, he called Pastor Rodney, totally surprised at the love and generosity he had been shown. Reinhard said, "I can't stop praying for you. Every time I drive in my car, I think about you and pray for you. Every time I lay in my bed or go to the kitchen, I'm thanking God for you and praying for you. I'm praying more for you and your ministry than I am for my own!"

Pastor Rodney gave out of the abundance of love that God had given him. That type of generosity was without any strings attached. Pastor Rodney didn't say, "If I give this to you, you need to pray for me." He wasn't looking for a wage or a payment for his gifts. He simply saw the story of the Shunammite woman in the Word and took it literally. He wanted to bless Reinhard Bonnke the same way the Shunammite had blessed Elisha. From that place, he gave abundant, generous gifts.

Sometime later, a pastor from Texas called Pastor Rodney and told him he had a gift for him. In fact, he was towing it to the church. Pastor Rodney was puzzled. What kind of gift needs to be towed? When he arrived, they were hauling a satellite dish assembly. It hit him then: This is what I need to reach the world with the Gospel without having to travel! That next year, Revival Ministries International ministered to more people than all the other years put together, and he was able to sleep in his own bed, drive in his own car, and live at home.

The Lord knew Pastor Rodney's desire to minister and reach the nations without traveling so much, and He placed the solution within the pastor's heart. In the same way, the Shunammite woman blessed a man of God and was blessed in return. When you give with radical love, you will receive radical love. The Lord loves a radical and cheerful giver (see 2 Cor. 9:7).

The only way that men of God like Pastor Rodney could have given such radical gifts was because he had experienced such a radical love from God. Worldly love always requires something in return, i.e., "I love you. Do you love me?" "I sacrificed my time for you; how will you repay me?" But God's love is unconditional. While we were enemies in our minds toward God, He came and died for us (see Rom. 5:8).

When we see and experience this deep love, we are then able to give it to others. They don't need to pay us back physically or emotionally. Then, we aren't acting in earthly love but moving in God's love. 1 John 4:19 says, "We love because He first loved us." It is impossible for you to love without first having received the love of God for yourself. When you realize that He came into your deepest, darkest sin and said, "I love you," it changes the way you do everything.

Peter says it like this, "...Add to your faith virtue, to virtue knowledge, to knowledge self-control, to self-control perseverance, to perseverance godliness, to godliness brotherly kindness, and to brotherly kindness love. For if these things are yours and abound, you will be neither barren nor unfruitful in the knowledge of our Lord Jesus Christ. For he who lacks these things is shortsighted, even to blindness, and has forgotten that he was cleansed from his old sins (see 2 Peter 1:5-9)."

If we lack love, it is because we have forgotten that we, too have been shown mercy and grace and have been forgiven and cleansed from our old sins. When we aren't able to love someone else, we need to take a look at ourselves. We must remember that we, too, were entrenched in our own sin when He came into our lives. God had mercy on us and brought us to Himself. Now we have the same opportunity and responsibility to see others in this way. His love has transformed us and will transform others. All we need to do is receive it boldly and give it to a lost world.

Meditation

"For here is the way God loved the world—he gave his only, unique Son as a gift. So now everyone who believes in him will never perish but experience everlasting life."

- John 3:16 (TPT)

How amazing is God's love for us? Think about the reality of God sending His very own Son to initiate a relationship with you! How does this show your value? Let the truth of God's radical love for you wash over your mind. That same love He has for you is now active inside of you. That same love wants to be expressed in the world around you. Who is God putting on your heart to express His love toward? How does He want you to express it? Notice that when you experience love, the natural outflow is to give.

Chapter Four

Love Transforms

The Bible says that we, the Church, are to be known for love. I've got bad news: The Church today is not known for love. It's better known for judgment, condemnation, and accusation. And we often live in a place of religiosity where we come against people for what they're doing wrong instead of building them up for what they're doing right! What's sad is we condemn the sinners in the world for sinning. They are sinners! They're not the righteousness of God. This is normal for them right now, so how could we expect anything different? That's like condemning an apple for not being an orange.

Unless we become love and show what righteousness looks like, the lost will never desire Him. However, if they do see it, they'll say, "Wow, is this what the family of God is like? I want what they have." What doesn't work is approaching them, saying, "You're wrong there, there, and there. You're living with your girlfriend. You're still drinking too much. When are you going to get this right?"

When we focus on actions as proof of transformation, we are inviting people into religion, not relationship. We are essentially using church-appropriate language to say, "prove yourself to me." That's what the Pharisees did. This mindset will only blind us. We will see people according to their performance and not according to their potential.

Jesus broke bread with sinners. Who did He come against? The Pharisees—the people who were enforcing the Law. Jesus said to them, "You brood of vipers. You whitewashed tombs" (see Matt. 23:27 and Matt. 23:33). Those aren't compliments. Jesus detested their religious practices and hypocrisy. They were constantly imposing unfair and impractical standards. They condemned the lost for their actions instead of showing mercy and empowering them to change.

We often focus so much on what a person *does* that we can't even see who they *are*. If no one ever believes in them, what will happen? They will stay in the cycle they're used to. How often do we, as believers, freak out when someone does something small compared to what our Bible heroes did? Again, I'm not justifying sin. But I find it interesting that when someone does something wrong, they are instantly condemned by those around them.

God regularly forgave people at their worst. Look at David's track record: Adultery. Lying. Murder. And what did God call him? "A man after My own heart" (see Acts 13:22). How about Abraham? "Now Abraham said of Sarah, his wife, 'She is my sister.' And Abimelech, king of Gerar, sent and took Sarah" (Gen. 20:2). Abraham lied multiple times but still made it into the Hebrews 11 "Hall of Faith"!

These are the people whose faith we look up to! We can't treat these biblical accounts as stories that have no relevance today. We have to place ourselves in their stories. What would it be like to be a person following Abraham or David's leadership? How would you respond when they failed? What would you do when you found out David committed adultery with one of his captain's wives and then killed him to cover it up? How do you feel God should respond? How does He? How does this change or confirm your understanding of how God is interacting with you today?

I encourage you, when you're in your darkest day and thinking, *Oh, I'm such a horrible, wicked, evil sinner*, to look through Scripture at some of the men and women who found favor with God. I'd say that most of you have probably done a better job. As I said before, I'm not justifying sin. Sin is sin, and it's wrong. But in order to live without sin, we have to recognize that God's love meets us where we are and empowers us to become who He has called us to be.

We are instructed in Scripture to love the lost because love *covers a multitude of sins* (see 1 Peter 4:8). Love believes the best, hopes the best, endures all things and never fails. We must understand this truth. It is time for us to be possessed by love. Then we will show the world *real* love. They will want more and more of it, and it will lead them right to the source: God Himself.

It's impossible for us to do this on our own. When we try, we're doing it out of self-righteousness. We have to become possessed by His love so that we can love others as He does. Not one time in the Bible do we see Jesus say to a sinner, "go clean up your life, and then we can talk." Consistently, Jesus' only statement to sinners seems to be, "Come and dine with me. Spend time with me."

Never once do we see Jesus demand transformation from any sinner, and yet, so many of those who interacted with Jesus were radically transformed. Zaccheus, the tax collector, paid back every dollar he had ever cheated. The Samaritan woman at the well, who had multiple failed marriages, became one of the first evangelists. Mary, the prostitute, broke the alabaster jar worth a year's wages to anoint Jesus. Jesus never demanded these things of them. They merely responded to the love He poured out on them in whatever way they could.

We don't need to tell the lost how lost they are. Most of the time, they already know. What they need to know more than anything is that they are loved right where they are, in the middle of their mess. It is the love of Jesus that transforms the world.

Meditation

"God didn't go to all the trouble of sending his Son merely to point an accusing finger, telling the world how bad it was. He came to help, to put the world right again."
- John 3:17 (MSG)

It is impossible to love others when we are pointing the finger at everything they've done wrong. As you meditate on this verse, ask the Lord to show you if there is anywhere you've closed off your heart toward the lost. Ask Him to soften those areas of your heart and show you His heart of love for them. If He brings to mind any accusations you've made, repent and release the judgment. Let His love wash over your mind and change how you think about yourself and everyone around you.

Chapter Five

Possessed by Love

"That Christ may dwell in your hearts through faith; that you, being rooted and grounded in love, may be able to comprehend with all the saints what is the width and length and depth and height—to know the love of Christ which passes knowledge; that you may be filled with all the fullness of God."
- Ephesians 3:17-19

How are you filled with the fullness of God? By knowing the love of Christ. Notice how this verse does not say, "To know your love *for* Christ." We tend to make it about us and *our* love for Him. But in reality, we can't love Him unless we experience His love for us first. That's why it says to know the love *of* Christ, not your love *for* Christ.

We make it about us and say things like, "How desperate are you? How hungry are you? Come on, cry out right now. You've got to go after this thing," instead of us experiencing His love and becoming possessed by it. His love is what changes everything. Our love for Him goes up and down. We're not always going to feel like we love Him. Some days we will say, "Oh Jesus, we love you," and other days, we think, *Oh, why are all these bad*

27

things happening; I don't feel like loving God today. Our love is not consistent, but His love for us is. It's always being poured out upon us. "And this hope will not lead to disappointment. For we know how dearly God loves us, because he has given us the Holy Spirit to fill our hearts with his love" (Rom. 5:5 NLT). His love has become the foundation of who we are.

When you're on a ship, and the constant up-down motion gets to you, what happens? You get seasick. Similarly, some of us get lost because of the up-and-down experience of our relationship with God. When you are seasick, what are you supposed to do? Look at the horizon. The sickness then leaves because your eyes are focused on something steady. Christ's love for you is consistent. It will never change. It doesn't go up and down. His love is like the horizon—always consistent.

This is why we have to be focused on His love for us every single day. That's what this is all about. It's not about telling people what they're doing right or wrong. Anyone can do that. It takes someone who is possessed by His love to manifest Jesus to the world around us.

Heidi Baker of Iris Ministries is one of the most recognized and well-known missionaries of our time. She has planted over 2,000 churches among the Makua people in Mozambique, a group labeled "nearly unreached.". She travels worldwide year after year, preaching the Gospel and sharing her experiences. However, the thing she is most known for is not church planting but her absolute love for the Lord and people. Her life is an example of one which has been possessed by love.

Several years ago, I had the opportunity to be one of her security at a conference. Our job was to escort her from the meeting to her hotel room each day. The hotel where she was staying was very nice and expensive. To add to it, the host church had booked her in the presidential suite. When she entered the room the first night, she was astounded by its size. As she looked around, she said, "I don't need this much space for myself. Why would I need all of this?"

After helping her settle in, we left for the night. When we arrived the next morning to take her back to the conference, what I saw marked me. After we left the night before, she had gone out on the streets. She had found a homeless woman and invited her to have a warm place to stay the night. She could not stand being in a large room by herself, knowing that people were sleeping outside on the freezing sidewalk.

Heidi is a very busy person. She travels all over the world, and when she's not traveling, she's on the mission field in Mozambique. She could have easily used the night in the presidential suite as a time to refresh and reset, but instead, she kept doing what she is known for—stopping for the "one."

There is no question that this homeless woman got a picture of what God's love for her looked like. She didn't have the money to afford any place to sleep that night, let alone a presidential suite. But God saw her where she was, out in the cold and needing help. He sent her someone possessed by His love who could bring her into an encounter with His love. People everywhere are questioning what God is like. When we are overtaken by what He's done for us, we can provide the response.

Love is the answer. As we learn to walk in love, we will become love to others. Being possessed by His love is how we become the light of the world. It would have been easy for Heidi to say, "This woman deserves to be on the streets because of her bad decisions." But that's not what love does. God's kindness leads us to repentance (see Rom. 2:4). It's not telling people what they've done wrong. It happens through showing others His goodness, grace, and love.

Meditation

"...(Love) It always protects, always trusts, always hopes, always perseveres. Love never fails..."
- 1 Corinthians 13:7-8 (NIV)

God's love toward you has never ceased, changed, or failed you. Instead, it has always protected you, hoped for your well-being and success, and has relentlessly pursued you. Begin to meditate on the ways that God has loved you. If you're having trouble thinking of times He has displayed His love, ask the Holy Spirit to help you. Let your heart be stirred to praise in knowing His love for you. Allow yourself to dwell on the reality of how loving He's been toward you.

Chapter Six

Loving Our Own

"By this all will know that you are My disciples, if you have love for one another."

- John 13:35

Love starts close to home. Scripture tells us that the clearest way the world will be able to see we are followers of Jesus is through the way we love one another. Our relationship with other believers is a witness to what we truly believe about the Lord. When our Grace Place team travels together, one of the most common things we hear is there is something different and refreshing about us. There is a closeness about us that truly feels like a family. Our love for one another has created a depth of relationship some people consider odd, but Biblically is normal.

We have spent most of this book discussing the power unlocked through the art of loving others like God loves us. For the next few pages, I want to talk from a different perspective. This chapter is going to discuss a few of the times we, as the Body of Christ, have gotten it wrong. To some of you, this sounds sharper than the rest of the book. But the fact of the matter is we are dealing with a lost world, and time is short.

Some of the clearest examples of how we lack selfless love can be found in how we respond to those who have fallen in ministry. How we, as the Body of Christ, have handled these scenarios is unsettling. When you look at well-known ministers who have stumbled and have gotten into horrible situations, we often see a church that has failed to cover a multitude of sins. We hang them out to dry, and we point the finger. We accuse and condemn, saying, "You don't deserve to be in this position." It's heartbreaking.

Many ministers have built huge churches and reached multitudes for the Gospel. But without knowing how to handle the publicity or pressure, they ended up in sin and compromise. I know someone who was directly involved in an extensive ministry where the leader was discovered to be living a secret life of compromise. The situation was not nearly as bad as the news made it sound, but it was definitely still sin. Regardless of how the facts were conveyed, how we, as the Body of Christ, handle situations like this is often heartbreaking.

This pastor started a church in his house, and it became one of the largest churches in America. He became one of the most influential pastors and leaders in the nation. Clearly, there was a gift from God on his life for leadership. So, how did the church handle his failure? They said, "Pastor, you'll never preach in this pulpit again." Many leaders publicly came out against him and accused him, saying things like, "How could you do this? How could you live your life like this?"

Do you know why a great percentage of our churches and leaders responded like this? It wasn't because we were concerned for the well-being of the Body of Christ. It wasn't because we saw the effects of his sin and wanted to protect those around us. It was because we were concerned about ourselves! It was because we were worried about what other people would think. We thought we would lose our credibility and that our integrity would be called into question. *Could my leader be capable of doing the same things? My pastor is friends with this man. I wonder if he was in on it?* We feared that if people knew we were close to him, or God forbid, that we even forgave his actions, our reputation would plummet. We became more concerned about ourselves than about loving this man who needed help.

The situation got worse. The house the pastor was living in was owned by his church. They called a meeting and decided that they could not have him living on church property. His church kicked him out of his own home with no place to go. That's not love. It got even worse.

Two major celebrities who are well-known for promoting sinful lifestyles reached out to him. They said, "Hey, we heard the church kicked you out of your house. We have a few spare houses if you'd like to stay in one of ours." Think about that. Two people in public lifestyles of sin who openly opposed godliness thought what the church did to its pastor was unjust. They opened up their extra homes to him. Again, I'm not promoting or excusing sin. However, don't you think it's sad that this man received more compassion from the world than he did from those who are called to preach redemption?

We have to wake up. We are one of the only groups of people in the world that attack our own wounded instead of covering them. Paul warns us in Galatians 5:15, saying, "If you bite and devour one another, beware lest you be consumed by one another!" The freedom we received in Christ was so we could love, not so we could sit as judges and punish people for their wrongdoing. It's time to wake up to what love is and show it to not just the world but to our own. When one of our leaders fails, we should cover them. We have to look out for them. We should remind them who they are in Christ. They need to be empowered to clean up their messes. Our focus should be their redemption, not their destruction.

There is a popular musical artist today who came from a Christian family and grew up in church. A number of years before this person became famous, they were called out by a prophet during a church service, who began to speak about their calling. He prophesied how they were going to be one of the most influential people in the entertainment industry and how God was going to use them to accomplish great things.

When all of this happened, this person was still young and undiscovered. The church prayed over them, blessed them, and sent them out. It was an anointed moment. Some time later, a talent agent found this person online. This agent paid for them to record their first album, which became a massive success almost overnight. The rest is history.

Here's what's sad. If I were to tell you this person's name, you'd probably recognize it. You can find videos of them doing worship sets, sharing about Jesus, and using their platform to spread the Gospel. However, their sin and mistakes have been broadcasted everywhere. I'm not justifying what they've done, but knowing the position that they're in and knowing all the challenges they regularly face, what has been the Church's response? Believers sat on the judgment seat, saying things like, "They did what? Smoking weed? Obviously, they're not a Christian."

We start condemning and accusing instead of saying, "Hmm. This person has roots. They have a history. Aspects of their lives are really going for God. So instead of accusing and condemning, I'm going to pray for this person, that God would apprehend their heart and that God's grace and love would come upon them. I pray that they would never stray away from everything they've been taught and trained in."

In John 9, the disciples, understanding that sin caused sickness, asked Jesus why a man was born blind. They wondered if it was the man's sin or his parents' sin that caused him to be blind. Jesus' response was not an answer to their question but an invitation to change their perspective. He said, "Neither this man nor his parents sinned, but that the works of God should be revealed in him" (v. 3). Religion trains us to always look for what was done wrong, but God is far more concerned about His glory and goodness being displayed.

Jesus didn't come only to reveal the sins of the world. He came to take them away. When we spend all of our time exposing people's sins rather than God's good work in their lives, we totally miss the ministry of love and reconciliation that Jesus came to demonstrate.

For the first time in history, we have people who can make a single post and influence huge portions of the world. When you look at all the influential people over the last few decades, you see that many started in the Church! Katy Perry's parents are prophetic ministers. Marcus Mumford, of the band Mumford and Sons, is the son of the leaders of the Vineyard Church in the U.K. Aretha Franklin started out singing gospel music. Beyoncé began singing in her church. Several others all grew up in Christian families. But when these people began to make mistakes and bad choices, the Church didn't choose love. Instead, it condemned them and drove them further away.

How do we welcome back in those who have strayed away? How can we help those who are fallen in ministry, and in need of restoration? The answer is always the same. Love them. We often overcomplicate things, thinking it takes something drastic. However, the road to restoration can begin with a simple phone call asking, "How are you? How can I help?"

We often worry about how our reputations might be affected if someone were to find out who we're associating with. However, the Lord made Himself of no reputation to come and give Himself for our restoration (see Phil. 2:7-10). He is the God who leaves the ninety-nine to chase after the one. Whenever we put aside our comfort and reputations to care for those who have strayed away, we are following in the footsteps of our Savior.

I believe that many of us struggle to show love toward others in the midst of their failures because we lack an understanding of how much we are loved despite our own failures. If we knew how loved we were, we would have a much different response to others. If we understood how forgiven we have been, we would have a much greater ability to forgive the person in front of us when they fail. Yes, God hates sin with a passion. But He loves sinners with an even greater passion. We never know the potential of the person standing right in front of us. God loves to take those the world has written off and use them for something great. Remember, we are dealing with the God who chose Saul, a man who persecuted and murdered Christians, to write two-thirds of the New Testament.

Meditation

"This love of which I speak is slow to lose patience—it looks for a way of being constructive..."
- 1 Corinthians 13:4 (J.B. Phillips)

Take a moment to think about how love is patient. It isn't looking for a reason to write people off for every mistake they make; it's continually looking for a way to help the other person. God loves us and doesn't lose His patience with our mistakes or failures. He's always looking to help us. Allow the Holy Spirit to guide you as you meditate on this verse. Is there someone He brings to mind that has been written off for their mistakes? If so, how can you help them? If no one comes to mind, what is the Lord revealing to you about love and who He is? As you receive His love for you and others, watch as you begin to see the world in a whole new light!

Chapter Seven

A New Commandment

In John 13, Jesus was nearing the time when He would be crucified. Scripture records what could have been Jesus' final words to His disciples before His death. Jesus chose to use this time to establish a new commandment.

"A new commandment I give to you, that you love one another; as I have loved you, that you also love one another. "
- John 13:34

To put it another way, Jesus was saying, "Examine the way I've loved you and love others the same way." The way we love each other is an indicator of our identity in Christ. There is something about the way we, as believers, love each other that sets us apart from all other people. People should be able to look at our lives and say, "That's a follower of Jesus. I can tell because they know how to love."

What I find most interesting about this commandment isn't just what Jesus said but the context in which He said it. Jesus taught His disciples about the importance of loving one another immediately after the unveiling of Judas as His betrayer and right before predicting Peter's denial. This teaching on love is sandwiched between Jesus' acknowledgment of two instances of betrayal.

Jesus, being the Son of God and continuously doing only what He saw the Father doing, knew that Judas was a betrayer from the start. He knew that Judas would be the person responsible for turning Him over to be crucified. John 6:64 says, "...For Jesus knew from the beginning who they were who did not believe, and who would betray him." Yet, Jesus still chose Judas as one of His disciples. Not just any disciple either, but an intimate friend and member of His inner circle of twelve. He selected him to travel with Him, learn from Him for three years, and even placed him in charge of the ministry finances. Knowing everything Jesus knew about Judas, he's not the kind of person I would choose to love and keep close to me. Would you?

Peter was the passionate and outspoken leader of the disciples. He was always the first to volunteer and the first to speak up. He was the only disciple documented as walking on water with Jesus, but Peter was going to fail and fail badly. In the moment of Jesus' greatest need for comfort and friendship, Peter would deny he even knew Him. When the pressure was put on Peter about whether or not he stood with Jesus, he found out he didn't. He chose self-protection and fear instead of connection. He chose to save himself instead of dying with Jesus like he always said he would.

Jesus knew all of this when He chose Peter! Certainly, it was on His mind the night He was betrayed. Yet, just like with Judas, Jesus didn't try to preserve Himself from people who would cause Him pain. He chose Peter, fully knowing the fact he would deny Him.

When Jesus said in John 13, "Love one another; as I have loved you, that you also love one another," is this what He meant? That in the same way that He chose connection and intimacy with people who had high potential to cause Him grief and harm, we should love the same way? And don't forget, *all* of the disciples fled when Jesus was arrested. At His crucifixion, only John was present.

But even knowing their failures, Jesus still chose them. After His resurrection, Jesus did not seek revenge or retribution against them. He went out of His way to comfort them and remind them that they were still chosen. How we treat someone on their worst day is a far better indicator of the quality of love we have than how we treat someone on their best day.

It's not hard to love someone who is treating you well. The world does that already. When we choose love for one another amid disappointment, pain, confusion, regret, remorse, or betrayal—that is the kind of love that makes the world take notice. It's not logical. When it feels like we have every right to take revenge, and yet we choose acceptance and love, we are living according to the new commandment.

Meditation

"A new commandment I give to you, that you love one another; as I have loved you, that you also love one another."

- John 13:34

How has God loved you? As you meditate on the scripture, list out some of the ways that God has shown up in your life. Think about a time you were at your worst, and He loved you anyway. Think of times when you thought God couldn't get better, but He did.

Ask the Holy Spirit, just as Paul does in Ephesians 3:16-18, that you would have the full strength and power to comprehend His love for you. As you experience it, you'll be changed into His likeness.

Conclusion

You were created in God's image, and God is love. He is the definition of love. This is who He is. Because He lives in you, you are no longer who you used to be. You can now become love too. Galatians 2:20 says, "I have been crucified with Christ; it is no longer I who live, but Christ lives in me..." It's no longer about who you were or what you used to do. *Love* is who you are. Because you've become one with Christ, you've become one with love. What's true of God's character is true of you. I would encourage you to go through 1 Corinthians 13 and put yourself into every line. Read it aloud like this:

I never give up.
I care more for others than for myself.
I don't want what I don't have.
I don't strut.
I don't have a swollen head.
I don't force myself on others.
I'm not always "me first."
I don't fly off the handle.
I don't keep score of the sins of others.
I don't revel when others beg.
I take pleasure in growing in the truth.

I put up with anything.

I trust God always.

I consistently look for the best.

I never look back, but I keep going to the end.

These things are all true of God because God is Love. God is patient, God is kind, and God keeps no record of wrongs. However, we must cease to see the separation between His nature and our own. The lost art of living in selfless love is directly connected to how we see ourselves. If we think we are "mere men" in a relationship with God, we will never fully manifest His love.

The truth is *you* are patient. *You* are kind. You don't envy, you aren't puffed up, and you don't behave rudely. You think no evil, you don't rejoice in iniquity, but you rejoice in the truth. Imagine what this means for your life and circumstances.

Allow God's lens of unconditional love to shape how you view other people. Every part of who you are is filled with the fullness of Christ. Every part of you has been created to see God's love in another person. Every part of you is full of the anointing. You are lacking nothing. The Bible says you have all things pertaining to life and godliness (see 2 Peter 1:3). You have the fullness of God inside of you (see Col. 2:9-10).

See the potential He's placed in you. If you even tapped into a fraction of His potential in you, you would never be the same. Your family would never be the same. Your church and your job would never be the same.

Let yourself be possessed by God's love. Being possessed by God is being possessed by love itself. If you choose to be consumed by love, it's going to radically transform others. People are going to say, "Wow, there's something different about you. Not only can you prophesy, not only can you perform miracles, but you know how to love."

Revelation 2 begins with Jesus talking to the angel of the church of Ephesus, commending the church for their many good deeds. They labored, toiled, persevered, exposed false prophets, and more. However, it wasn't all good news. "But I have this against you, that you have left your first love. Therefore remember from where you have fallen, and repent and do the deeds you did at first." (Rev. 2:4-5 NASB).

Can you imagine hearing these words? What if you spent your whole life doing great things but missed the most important thing of all—being in love with Jesus? No matter how many good things we do, it will never take the place of being known and loved by the Lord. It's only when we know how loved we are that we can love the world around us.

It's time that we, as His body, return to the things we did at first. It's time we remember how it felt when we first experienced the joy of our salvation. We must remember how lost we would be without Him. Otherwise, we will never truly understand how desperate the world around us is to know Him.

Selfless love is not something we can achieve on our own strength. Without His love to fuel us, we will always be plagued by selfishness, agendas, distractions, worldly comforts, etc. Love is a spiritual gift that only grows by the power of the Holy Spirit. Without the Spirit to empower us, this will remain a lost art.

We are called to be the hands and feet of Jesus. We are alive to display the Father to the world. It would be tragic if, in our generation, we became experts in ministry giftings but missed the whole reason we are living. If we give our lives to make all the best churches, programs, and worship songs, but we did it all without love for the world and the lost, we've accomplished nothing. The Gospel is simple. Jesus died for us so we could live. This is what living out of love looks like. The most influential thing any one of us can do is become like Jesus and learn to live and love as He did.

When we do, we won't have to convince the world we are believers. They will know it already by our love for one another and those who are lost. They will see it and want to experience it. It's time we learn to love the world around us the way God loves us.

It's time for selfless love.

1 Corinthians 13 Translations

THE PASSION TRANSLATION

Love is large and incredibly patient. Love is gentle and consistently kind to all. It refuses to be jealous when blessing comes to someone else. Love does not brag about one's achievements nor inflate its own importance.

Love does not traffic in shame and disrespect, nor selfishly seek its own honor. Love is not easily irritated or quick to take offense. Love joyfully celebrates honesty and finds no delight in what is wrong.

Love is a safe place of shelter, for it never stops believing the best for others. Love never takes failure as defeat, for it never gives up. Love never stops loving...

THE MESSAGE

Love never gives up.
Love cares more for others than for self.
Love doesn't want what it doesn't have.
Love doesn't strut,
Doesn't have a swelled head,
Doesn't force itself on others,

Isn't always "me first,"
Doesn't fly off the handle,
Doesn't keep score of the sins of others,
Doesn't revel when others grovel,
Takes pleasure in the flowering of truth,
Puts up with anything,
Trusts God always,
Always looks for the best,
Never looks back,
But keeps going to the end.

JB PHILLIPS TRANSLATION

This love of which I speak is slow to lose patience—it looks for a way of being constructive.

It is not possessive: it is neither anxious to impress nor does it cherish inflated ideas of its own importance.

Love has good manners and does not pursue selfish advantage.

It is not touchy. It does not keep account of evil or gloat over the wickedness of other people.

On the contrary, it is glad with all good men when truth prevails.

Love knows no limit to its endurance, no end to its trust, no fading of its hope; it can outlast anything.

It is, in fact, the one thing that still stands when all else has fallen.

THE AMPLIFIED

Love endures with patience and serenity, love is kind and thoughtful, and is not jealous or envious; love does not brag and is not proud or arrogant.

It is not rude; it is not self-seeking, it is not provoked [nor overly sensitive and easily angered]; it does not take into account a wrong endured.

It does not rejoice at injustice, but rejoices with the truth [when right and truth prevail].

Love bears all things [regardless of what comes], believes all things [looking for the best in each one], hopes all things [remaining steadfast during difficult times], endures all things [without weakening].

Love never fails [it never fades nor ends].

NEW INTERNATIONAL VERSION

Love is patient, love is kind.

It does not envy, it does not boast, it is not proud.

It does not dishonor others, it is not self-seeking, it is not easily angered, it keeps no record of wrongs.

Love does not delight in evil but rejoices with the truth.

It always protects, always trusts, always hopes, always perseveres.

Love never fails...

NEW LIVING TRANSLATION

Love is patient and kind.
Love is not jealous or boastful or proud or rude.
It does not demand its own way.
It is not irritable, and it keeps no record of being wronged.
It does not rejoice about injustice but rejoices whenever the truth wins out.
Love never gives up, never loses faith, is always hopeful, and endures through every circumstance.

GOOD NEWS TRANSLATION

Love is patient and kind;
it is not jealous or conceited or proud;
love is not ill-mannered or selfish or irritable;
love does not keep a record of wrongs;
love is not happy with evil, but is happy with the truth.
Love never gives up; and its faith, hope, and patience never fail.

ABOUT GRACE PLACE

Grace Place Ministries is a discipleship community fueled by a passion to see God's people walk out their identity in Christ and establish His Kingdom upon the earth. We are committed to developing mature Christian leaders through one-on-one mentoring, building family through weekly gatherings, and providing leadership opportunities designed to facilitate connection and growth. We travel frequently to minister around the world and create resources to build up the Church in her righteous identity.

——————————

VISION

Mature sons and daughters
established in their identity in Christ,
spreading the Gospel of grace and truth.

MISSION

Disciple young adults.
Minister around the world.
Resource the nations.

Discipleship is our Mission; Will you Join Us?

Now, more than ever, the body of Christ needs to arise and shine. The world is searching for answers and is in need of an encounter with God's love and truth. Who will raise up a generation to bring answers our world is desperately seeking?

"For the earnest expectation of the creation eagerly waits for the revealing of the sons of God."
– Romans 8:19

Whether it is a young man or woman needing a mentor or an entire church seeking the resources to disciple their community, you can make an impact!

Become a Partner with Grace Place Ministries:

Go to:
WWW.GRACEPLACEPARTNER.COM

Grace Place Ministries

THE LOST ART OF DISCIPLESHIP
God's Model for Transforming the World

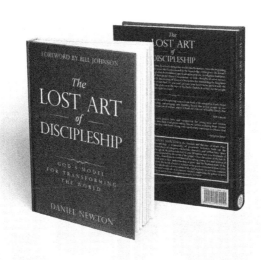

Discipleship is not a man-made idea. It is God's design for world transformation. *The Lost Art of Discipleship* is the uncovering of heaven's blueprints for remodeling the kingdoms of the earth into the Kingdom of our God. In his cornerstone book, Daniel Newton pulls from 20 years of experience in discipleship. As you read, prepare your heart to be ignited with the fires of revival that once swept the globe as in the days of the Early Church. It is time for the people of God to arise and shine for our light has come!

Available at www.GracePlaceMedia.com
@GracePlaceDiscipleship

Additional Resources

The Lost Art of Discipleship
Workbook

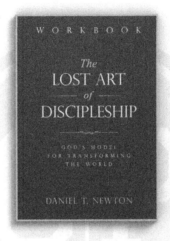

Enrich your understanding and increase your mastery of God's model for world transformation. This companion workbook to *The Lost Art of Discipleship* book is filled with exclusive content, in-depth exercises, and practical coaching to introduce a lifestyle of discipleship in your day-to-day walk. Whether you have been following the Lord for years or recently surrendered your life to Jesus, this manual breaks down the Great Commission and equips you for a life of fruitfulness!

Available at www.GracePlaceMedia.com
@GracePlaceDiscipleship

ADDITIONAL RESOURCES

THE LOST ART OF DISCIPLESHIP
Online Course

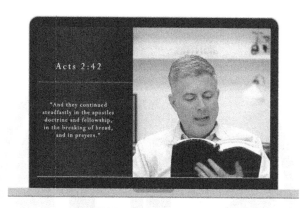

You can live the Great Commission. Every believer is called to embrace Jesus' final command: to make disciples... and this interactive online course is designed to take you even deeper into the rich content taught in *The Lost Art of Discipleship*.

Whether you are wanting to position yourself as a son or daughter, lead as a father or mother, or create a culture of discipleship, this course is for you! Rediscover the lost art with over five hours of video content, practical teaching, quizzes, and supernatural activations from Daniel Newton.

Available at www.GracePlaceMedia.com
@GracePlaceDiscipleship

ADDITIONAL RESOURCES

IMMEASURABLE
Reviewing the Goodness of God

You are made in the image of the Miracle Worker,
designed to manifest His glorious nature.
Immeasurable: Reviewing the Goodness of God is a collection
of 100 real-life stories of salvation, healing, deliverance,
signs and wonders, reconciliation, and provision. Every
miracle is a prophetic declaration of what God wants to
do in, through, and for someone just like you.

Available at www.GracePlaceMedia.com
@GracePlaceDiscipleship

ADDITIONAL RESOURCES

TRUTH IN TENSION
55 DAYS TO
Living in Balance

NEVER GIVE UP
The Supernatural Power of
Christ-like Endurance

Other Titles

THE LOST ART OF PERSEVERANCE
Rediscover God's Perspective on Your Trials

ALL THINGS
Have Become New, Work Together for Good, Are Possible

IT IS FINISHED
Exposing the Conquered Giants of Fear, Pride, and Condemnation

THE LOST ART OF FAITH RIGHTEOUSNESS
Rediscover How Believing Leads to Receiving

THE LOST ART OF FASTING
Cultivating a Deeper Hunger for God

Available at www.GracePlaceMedia.com

@GracePlaceDiscipleship

ADDITIONAL RESOURCES

GP MUSIC: BEGINNINGS

Everyone has a story. Most people don't realize that God doesn't just want to improve their story. He wants to rewrite it. Beginnings offers a fresh start, a new focus. This worship album invites you into the core anthems of grace and truth which have impacted us at Grace Place.

Our prayer is that this album helps you lay down your past mistakes, your present circumstances, and your future worries in order to lift both hands high in surrender to the One you were created to worship. We ask that you join us in a new beginning — an exciting start to a life filled with perseverance, focus, and surrender.

Available at www.GracePlaceMedia.com

@GracePlaceDiscipleship

KEEP US UPDATED

We would love to connect with you and hear about everything God has done in your life while reading this book! We also would love to hear how we can be praying for you. Submit a testimony or prayer request by going to www.GracePlaceRedding.com/mytestimony

STAY CONNECTED WITH GRACE PLACE

Are you interested in staying up to date with Grace Place Ministries and receiving encouraging resources via email?

VISIT OUR WEBSITE:
www.GracePlaceRedding.com

SIGN UP FOR OUR NEWSLETTER AT:
www.GracePlaceRedding.com/newsletter

FOLLOW US ON SOCIAL MEDIA:
@GracePlaceDiscipleship